MEDITATIONS ON M*A*S*H

KEEP MOVING!

JIM MARSHALL

TRILOGY
A WHOLLY OWNED SUBSIDARY OF **TBN**

PROFESSIONAL PUBLISHING MEETS POWERFUL PROMOTION

Trilogy Christian Publishers

A Wholly Owned Subsidiary of Trinity Broadcasting Network

2442 Michelle Drive

Tustin, CA 92780

Copyright © 2024 by Jim Marshall.

All Scripture quotations, unless otherwise noted are taken from The Living Bible copyright © 1971. Used by permission of Tyndale House Publishers, a Division of Tyndale House Ministries, Carol Stream, Illinois 60188. All rights reserved.

Scripture quotations marked MSG are taken from *THE MESSAGE,* copyright (c) 1993, 2002, 2018 by Eugene H. Peterson. Used by permission of NavPress. All rights reserved. Represented by Tyndale House Publishers, Inc.

Scripture quotations marked NLT are taken from the Holy Bible, New Living Translation, copyright © 1996, 2004, 2015 by Tyndale House Foundation. Used by permission of Tyndale House Publishers, Inc., Carol Stream, Illinois 60188. All rights reserved.

Scripture quotations marked "Phillips" are taken from The New Testament in Modern English, copyright 1958, 1959, 1960 J.B. Phillips and 1947, 1952, 1955, 1957 The Macmillian Company, New York. Used by permission. All rights reserved.

Scripture quotations taken from the 21st Century King James Version®, copyright © 1994. Used by permission of Deuel Enterprises, Inc., Gary, SD 57237. All rights reserved.

Scripture quotations marked (KJV) taken from The Holy Bible, King James Version. Cambridge Edition: 1769.

All rights reserved, including the right to reproduce this book or portions thereof in any form whatsoever.

For information, address Trilogy Christian Publishing

Rights Department, 2442 Michelle Drive, Tustin, CA 92780.

Trilogy Christian Publishing/ TBN and colophon are trademarks of Trinity Broadcasting Network.

For information about special discounts for bulk purchases, please contact Trilogy Christian Publishing.

Trilogy Disclaimer: The views and content expressed in this book are those of the author and may not necessarily reflect the views and doctrine of Trilogy Christian Publishing or the Trinity Broadcasting Network.

10 9 8 7 6 5 4 3 2 1

Library of Congress Cataloging-in-Publication Data is available.

ISBN 979-8-89041-824-1

ISBN 979-8-89041-825-8 (ebook)

ACKNOWLEDGMENTS

I have been a fan of the *M.A.S.H* TV show for many years. Having seen each episode multiple times, I still enjoy watching this once in a lifetime series.

My love for *M.A.S.H* has been supported and shared by my wonderful wife, Marg, and my four children—Hyperion, Landon, Saralyn, and Jaime. They have watched and laughed with me over many happy hours.

I also want to thank many others who have encouraged me in writing this book. Special thanks go out to Butch and Phyllis Barnhart, John and Lisa Unger, Buddy Nelms, Carol Jo Hahn, Tom and Roberta Hurt, Randy Dudding, and Tom Jones, who have prayed and supported me in this project.

I am grateful for my sister, Tammy Edwards, who has edited this book and encouraged me from the start.

TABLE OF CONTENTS

Description of Key Characters 11

The Scope of Each Meditation 13

A Controlled Response 15

A Rude Awakening 17

A Tale of Two Men 19

Adjustment 21

Advancement 23

All Behavior Is Caused 25

An Unperson 27

Assuming 29

Bad Reports 33

Being a Safety Net 35

Big Cheese 37

A Break in the Gloom 39

Sometimes You Hear the Bullet 41

Can't We All Get Along? 43

Change 45

Crisis 47

Don't Believe Everything You Read. 49

Who Gets the Credit? 51

Trading Places. 53

Time to Choose 55

Farewells. 57

Filling Big Shoes. 59

Fudging the Numbers 61

Tiered Miracles 63

The Smell of Music. 65

I Need Your Hep 67

It Will All Work Out 69

The Same Team. 71

Jumping On the Wagon. 73

5 'O Clock Charlie 75

The Rumor Mill 77

Get Back to Work 79

Growing Up 81

The Right Time 83

Keep Moving 85

The Law of the Harvest. 87

The Race of Life	89
Left Behind	91
That's the Problem, We Don't Know	93
The Kids	95
Moving Out of Our Comfort Zone	97
New Ways of Seeing	99
Obligations	101
Ownership	103
Passing the Buck	105
Taking Advantage	107
The Blame Game	109
The Challenge Of Command	111
Hidden Heroes	113
One Step More	115
Endnote	117

DESCRIPTION OF KEY CHARACTERS

Hawkeye Pierce (Alan Alda)
Chief Surgeon of M.A.S.H 4077.
In many of the stories he is the main star.

BJ Hunnicut (Mike Farrel)
Fellow surgeon working alongside Hawkeye. These two characters drive the show with their antics and escapades.

Captain John McIntyre (Trapper)
Preceded BJ Hunnicut as sidekick surgeon with Captain Pierce. Trapper was a real "cut up," no pun intended.

Colonel Potter (Harry Morgan)
Commanding Officer of MASH 4077. Older than other personnel, he tries to be a friend as well as a boss.

Lieutenant Colonel Henry Blake (McLean Stevenson)
First Commanding Officer of MASH 4077. Though somewhat inept and non-commanding, he is highly relational.

Major Frank Burns (Larry Linville)
A gung-ho doctor who eats and sleeps military regulations. He is in a sneak-around-your-back relationship with Major Margaret Houlihan.

Major Charles Winchester (David Ogden Stiers)
> A highly skilled doctor from Boston who is often pitted against Hawkeye and BJ.

Major Margaret Houlihan (Loretta Swit)
> Known as "Hot Lips," she commands the nurses of M.A.S.H 4077.

Radar O'Reilly (Gary Burghoff)
> Company clerk of MASH 4077. The entire unit depends on this "Iowa Boy" to keep things running.

Klinger (Jamie Farr)
> Follows Radar as company clerk. A fast talking, ever scheming to get out of the army guy from Toledo, Ohio.

Father Mulcahy (William Christopher)
> Chaplain of the unit. A very sincere person who tries to make a difference. He usually is easy going and is part of the colonel's inner circle.

Major Sidney Freeman (Allan Arbus)
> A travelling psychiatrist who likes the 4077 unit and its personnel.

THE SCOPE OF EACH MEDITATION

A major strength of each *M.A.S.H* show is the writing. Obviously, the actors are tremendous, but they can only portray what is written for them.

Each episode has multiple subplots which can stand on their own. However, the focus in these meditations is to deal with only one plot.

This will assist those who know the show and others who are new to it.

A CONTROLLED RESPONSE

Season 6, Episode 5

SCENARIO

Major Sidney Freeman visits the 4077, not as a psychiatrist, but as a patient, due to a head injury he sustained. While in camp he sees several of the staff who all seem to be dealing with "someof the crazy."

Tensions mount—Colonel Potter gives permission to build a bonfire. The pile grows and grows as more items are chosen. The match is struck, and a sort of calm comes as the flames burn high into the night sky.

OBSERVATION

Most of us are not directly involved in war, but our stress-filled lives can sometimes approximate a battlefield. Tensions build and pressures must be released before there is an explosion.

Finding our controlled response usually comes after trial and error. We can't always burn our excess junk or run away and hide. But, we can take a break now and then from the overload in our lives by:

- Ceasing, for a while, from the daily news.

- Getting off social media for as long as needed.
- Being out in nature, allowing it to restore your sense of well-being.
- Letting others share your load and laugh together.

Someone said, "the first one hundred years are the hardest," and so they are.

"I am leaving you with a gift—peace of mind and heart! And the peace I give isn't fragile like the peace the world gives. So don't be troubled or afraid" (John 14:27).

A RUDE AWAKENING

Season 2, Episode 9

SCENARIO

A soldier arrives needing blood but is worried he might get the "wrong color" of blood when he sees some African American personnel, including a nurse, who is an officer.

To teach this prejudiced man a lesson, Hawkeye and Trapper apply a tincture of iodine solution to this guy's head and hands while he is sedated. It darkens his skin, and when he awakens, he is agitated about his new look. All the staff play along with the prank, which only intensifies the man's fear. It's a hard lesson, but he learns we all bleed the same.

OBSERVATION

All of us carry some form of prejudice, whether it be towards people, food, or a place of origin. Much of this comes from how we were raised. If our parents were small-minded, preferring to see things from only their perspective, chances are we act the same way.

It's a big, growin' up day when we discover that some things which we thought surely were right are wrong. Our narrowness of mind and experience tends to imprison our thinking and keep us oblivious to greater realities.

Questioning your own belief system is not a threat, but an honest way to maintain a life worth living.

> *"Here is a simple rule of thumb for behavior:*
> *Ask yourself what you want people to do for you;*
> *then grab the initiative and do it for them!"*
> *(Luke 6:31, MSG).*

A TALE OF TWO MEN

Season 9, Episode 18

SCENARIO

Two army buddies arrive at the 4077 with different injuries. One, named Sturgis, wants to give his blood to his friend Dan. In checking the blood of Sturgis for compatibility, the doctors discover leukemia.

Captain Pierce has to tell Sturgis he has leukemia. Father Mulcahy quickly discovers his challenge of meeting the Cardinal pales in light of a patient basically being told he is terminal.

Even after knowing of the leukemia, Sturgis still is thinking only of his buddy, wanting to stay with him as long as possible.

The Father's morning sermon is totally changed as he confesses his own selfishness compared to the patient's unselfishness for his brother-in-arms.

OBSERVATION

Self-preservation is as natural as breathing. We protect ourselves and make decisions according to how it impacts us. Our worries and concerns become the driver of our lives.

To love and care for others at our own expense is difficult, to say the least. It does not happen by accident, but is a deliberate, ongoing decision. Since everyone we meet is carrying some kind of burden weighing them down, it is imperative that we move beyond our own maladies and focus on the needs of others. By doing so, our own troubles lighten.

> *"There is no greater love than to lay down one's life for one's friends" (John 15:13, NLT).*

ADJUSTMENT

Season 4, Episode 8

SCENARIO

Colonel Potter begins his service as C.O. (Commanding Officer) of the 4077 M.A.S.H. (Mobile Army Surgical Hospital). He writes his wife, Mildred, to describe it.

Radar wants to please his new boss but finds it hard to adjust to a new commander. Margaret and Frank take pictures of the C.O. and hire a local artist to make a bust of the colonel as an anniversary present.

Radar, BJ, and Hawkeye rescue a horse, and Radar gives it to the colonel. Being an ex-cavalry man, he is overwhelmed by the generous gift of the mare.

OBSERVATION

Adjusting to a new work environment as well as a total change in coworkers is usually quite intimidating. Learning personalities and inside information reinforces the idea you are the "new kid on the block." Dealing with this level of "newness" will take time and patience, especially with yourself.

Not all work situations demonstrate generosity and

kindness to the "new person." So you may have to model the kind of behavior you want. It's okay to shower others with thoughtful gifts—what goes out will return in due time. Reward your team by adjusting to them first. Example is still the best teacher.

> *"It is God himself who has made us what we are and given us new lives from Christ Jesus; and long ages ago he planned that we should spend these lives helping others" (Ephesians 2:10).*

ADVANCEMENT

Season 5, Episode 4

SCENARIO

Radar wins a card game with the doctors. As the game breaks up, a visiting sergeant tries to leave but owes Hawkeye and BJ for past games. Not being able to pay his debt, a deal is struck with the sergeant to manipulate the paperwork, thereby causing Radar to receive a promotion from a corporal to a Second Lieutenant. No one can believe it, especially Radar.

Adjusting to his new rank is not what he expected. Old friends don't accept his new authority and other officers are very skeptical. Finally, the docs are able to get the orders reversed and Radar returns to his former status.

OBSERVATION

It's easy, almost automatic, to believe we'd be happier if we're elevated to a higher position, thereby increasing our income and having others do the mundane tasks we've had to do. We're moving up—it's a new day.

Understand, things are not always what they seem to be. We look at others and imagine what it would be like to walk in their shoes, oblivious to the pressures and responsibilities they carry.

Wanting to advance, to fulfill our destiny, is a good thing. Complacency always derails dreams.

On the other hand, contentment makes the journey smoother, like oil does for an engine. Yes, we might not get there as fast, but when we do, we will not be worn out but have some left in the tank.

> *"Don't you realize that everyone runs, but only one person gets the prize? So run to win!"*
> *(1 Corinthians 9:24, NLT).*

ALL BEHAVIOR IS CAUSED

Season 8, Episode 21

SCENARIO

Sgt. Michael Yee, an Asian-American, arrives at the 4077 in desperate need of medical help. The doctors do a good job and the sergeant is on the mend. However, his injuries are serious enough to send him home for good. He is no longer mentally and emotionally fit for combat.

The sergeant slashes his wrists in a suicide attempt. Dr. Sidney Freeman, a psychiatrist, is brought in to treat the sergeant. Under hypnosis it is discovered this combat veteran, for the first time in his career, is fighting against people who look like him—he feels like a man with no country. He is given a non-threatening substitute action of twitching his hand whenever he feels guilty, which allows him to heal.

OBSERVATION

All behavior is caused. There are reasons why we do certain things, why we like or dislike things. Our past triggers memories or warnings about what is pleasant or even harmful to us, and we act accordingly.

No one is exempt from this reality. We all behave in ways, at times, which surprise others. Running on false guilt will eventually leave you stranded.

> *"But God put his love on the line for us by offering his Son in sacrificial death while we were of no use whatever to him" (Romans 5:8, MSG).*

AN UNPERSON

Season 4, Episode 5

SCENARIO

Hawkeye and BJ are awakened at 2:00 a.m. with a call from Hawk's dad requesting to speak with BJ, Hawkeye's fellow surgeon. The person calling asks HOW and WHY before the line is cut. Dr. Pierce waits nervously for his dad to call back.

Meanwhile, Lt. Digger, from the morgue detail, shows up to collect Dr. Pierce's body since, according to army records, he has been reported to have died. The lieutenant explains why the death certificate was sent to Hawk's dad—hence, the phone call. For a while, Dr. Pierce gets no mail or pay since the army thinks he is dead.

Hawk gets on the morgue bus to leave, since he is considered dead anyway. After seriously thinking about what is happening and getting fifty feet down the road, the doctor gets off and goes back to the operating room to deal with the new wave of casualties.

OBSERVATION

In George Orville's novel *1984*, he states that a person who has been erased from official records becomes an "unperson."

Statistical snafus happen all the time. If one happens to you, what do you do? Hawkeye chose, temporarily, to abdicate all responsibility, since he was considered dead. Why keep trying to make a difference if you get no credit and no pay?

The feeling of being an "unperson" is more prevalent than we think. While we are still counted in some manner, we may feel lost in the numbers, just another statistic living in quiet desperation.

Good news! Feelings are fickle and short-lived. You were placed here on earth for a reason. Until that purpose is accomplished, you shouldn't try to check out early—you would leave a world of hurt.

> *"There's an opportune time to do things, a right time for everything on the earth: a right time for birth and another for death"*
> *(Ecclesiastes 3:1–2, MSG).*

ASSUMING

Season 10, Episode 7

SCENARIO

The 4077 is cut off from the world due to a snafu in the U.S. Postal Service that disrupts delivery of second-class mail overseas. However, wealthy Major Winchester receives a package from home with seven newspapers of the Boston Globe. (This paper, apparently, only travels first class.)

The major's hope was to keep his windfall private, but soon his precious newsprint is discovered. A plan is announced to share each day's paper with the camp only after the major has first perusal. This went okay the first day but then blew up when Winchester, not finding his second-day paper, assumed it was stolen. He immediately ended the reading plan, scolding and belittling his fellow soldiers, which only intensified their resentment of him.

The third-day Boston Globe explained the reason day two was missing—a wildcat truckers' strike (one taken by unionized workers without approval of their union leader) prevented the paper from being delivered that day. However, the major failed to read ahead, so he blamed his comrades in arms.

OBSERVATION

Assuming things about others is as old as creation. Too often we excuse it as "that's just the way they are." Very seldom does it start out positively, and it usually exhibits in a negative manner.

Selfishness appears to be the driving force behind this behavior. If left unchecked, it can escalate to violence.

So, how do we begin giving others the benefit of the doubt?

1. **Get an attitude change.** This ultimately begins by recognizing God assumed the best of us, so He sent His Son to redeem us, giving us a way to live positively. Knowledge alone is not enough. Forgiveness must dominate the equation.

2. **Periodic checkups**—treating others with respect and dignity is a daily decision. It is so easy to slide into the world's way of thinking that what is yours is mine if I can take it. This includes reputation.

3. **Living by the Golden Rule is never out of style.**
Treating others the way we want to be treated will change the atmosphere of your world. So many times you've been given the benefit of the doubt. It's time to pass it on.

"But God put his love on the line for us by offering

his Son in sacrificial death while we were of no use whatever to him" (Romans 5:8, MSG).

BAD REPORTS

Season 6, Episode 23

SCENARIO

Colonel Potter is called to Headquarters to discover bad reports are coming from someone inside his M.A.S.H unit. Meanwhile, people at the 4077 are preparing to celebrate the Kentucky Derby they will hear on the radio.

Colonel Potter returns upset at the bad reports about himself and breaks up the party. Hawkeye and BJ confront the colonel, demanding to know why he is acting out against them. He shares about the negative reports and states he is going home.

Outgoing mail is checked, discovering a young corpsman had been sent as a spy by a disgruntled colonel who had not received preferential treatment while a patient at the 4077. The inner circle, Hawkeye, BJ, and Radar, plead for Potter to stay. The colonel, rather reluctantly, decides to stay.

OBSERVATION

It's never easy to receive criticism, yet if you're breathing, you will be criticized. So how will you handle it? Like Colonel Potter, you may choose to run away. Or, you could stay and fight to clear your name.

When you are criticized, consider the following:

- While much of the criticism is inflated and often untrue, still, some of it may be valid. Be prepared to own up and make changes.
- Understand that those who find fault with you do not know all the facts and issues.
- Most faults can be made right by honest reflection and course correction.
- Allow personal criticism to curb your own fault finding.

"Since I know it is all for Christ's good, I am quite happy about 'the thorn,' and about insults and hardships, persecutions and difficulties; for when I am weak, then I am strong—the less I have, the more I depend on him" (2 Corinthians 12:10).

BEING A SAFETY NET

Season 9, Episode 13

SCENARIO

Colonel Horace Balwin, visits the 4077 (the same man who sent Winchester to this unit just to get out of paying the money he lost to the major in cribbage).

When Winchester hears of the visit, he begins to plan revenge. Klinger intervenes and tells the major to treat the visiting colonel royally, even letting him win at cribbage.

Colonel Baldwin asks Winchester to arrange for a female to come to his tent late at night, promising him reassignment to Tokyo in return. By mistake, Margaret goes to the colonel's tent to deliver some papers. The colonel thinks she has come to entertain him. She screams in disgust upon finding the colonel in the dark tent wearing a hood.

The colonel accuses Margaret of moral impropriety and requests Winchester to side with him. Winchester, however, lets everyone know the colonel is lying through his teeth, thereby insuring Margaret's integrity.

OBSERVATION

There is a high cost to guarding the reputation of others. For Charles, it meant giving up the cushy job in the cultural city of Tokyo.

Unfortunately, the scenario described is more prevalent than we would like to acknowledge. We can easily find ourselves in a situation where we can slightly obscure the truth about a coworker or family member, which may benefit us.

Sometimes it's described as "maintaining morale" or "taking one for the team."

Safely guarding your own reputation is paramount in protecting others. In other words, you must be believable if you expect anyone to trust what you say. Payback will come in this life or the next, maybe sooner than you think.

"If you must choose, take a good name rather than great riches; for to be held in loving esteem is better than silver and gold"

(Proverbs 22:1).

BIG CHEESE

Season 3, Episode 21

SCENARIO

Word comes that General Douglas McArthur, supreme commander during the Korean Conflict, is planning to visit the 4077 due to its exemplary medical record.

An advance colonel arrives to instruct the staff on what to expect and how to act during the General's time with them. Extraordinary preparation begins to gear up for the visit. The camp does a mock practice of the general's arrival, with Radar playing the part of McArthur. However, without warning, the dignitary arrives early, unannounced. Rather than stopping, the general's entourage drives on through with just a cursory glance from McArthur as he does paperwork in his vehicle.

OBSERVATION

If you've lived any time at all, you know that promises often under deliver. In other words, we can get all excited about an event or happening, but when it actually arrives, it rarely lives up to the hype. It's not that anyone meant to disappoint but communication can easily break down. (Someone didn't get the memo, text, or call.)

So what do we do when these things happen? First of all, understand that even though we prepare for the best, sometimes it does not arrive on time, or even at all. Being mentally aware diminishes disappointment.

Secondly, do not neglect preparation. Getting ready for something is where we gain experience, especially when we do it with others. This cannot happen if we approach a project half-heartedly.

Lastly, keep your eye on the big picture. Details are necessary, but futile, if we do not know what the final product looks like or does. How we respond to unrealized expectations will greatly influence how we navigate the future.

> *"So be strong and courageous! Do not be afraid and do not panic before them. For the* LORD *your God will personally go ahead of you. He will neither fail you nor abandon you"*
> *(Deuteronomy 31:6, NLT).*

A BREAK IN THE GLOOM

Season 9, Episode 2

SCENARIO

Day after day, it has been raining hard in Korea, causing the medical personnel to be depressed and listless.

Hawkeye receives some letters from a class of fifth graders in his hometown in Maine. Each student was assigned by a teacher friend of Captain Pierce to write a soldier and ask about his or her life.

So Hawkeye passes out the letters to the inner circle (Col. Potter, Capt. BJ Hunnicutt, Maj. Margaret Houlihan, Chaplain Mulcahy, and Maj. Winchester). The questions posed by the children are not easy and cause some soul searching, especially for Hawkeye. The rain continues as each soldier struggles to respond to the letter given to him or her.

The show ends with each letter being honestly answered and the cessation of rain. There is a break in the gloom, both externally and internally. The lift we often need comes more quickly when we focus on others.

OBSERVATION

Weather affects our moods, especially when it confines us to inside activities. Pointed questions, even from a stranger, can challenge our memory and cause us to revisit unsettled issues. On the positive side, these challenges can help us gain new perspective on past events. People and situations that we did not understand at the time are seen in a new light. The lift we often need comes more quickly when we focus on others.

> *"Tough times don't last, but tough people do"*
> *(Bob Schuller).* [1]

SOMETIMES YOU HEAR THE BULLET

Season 1, Episode 17

SCENARIO

An old grade school friend of Captain Pierce, Tommy, drops by the 4077 for a brief visit. His background as a correspondent now helps him as he is serving in an infantry unit, researching a new book he is writing entitled *You Never Hear the Bullet.*

Tommy goes back to the battle but soon returns critically wounded. Hawkeye cannot save him on the operating table.

Meanwhile, an underage soldier whom Dr. Pierce promised not to expose is trying to escape the 4077 to rejoin the war. Since Hawk could not save Tommy, he breaks his promise to the fifteen-year-old private and orders him placed under guard until he can be shipped home.

OBSERVATION

Most of us will never have to make life and death choices as, depicted in this *MASH* episode. True, we cannot save everyone we know, however, we can and must intervene in the lives of others when we see them going the wrong way and flirting with unseen danger.

Obviously, this is not an easy task. We risk alienation and anger from the person we're trying to help. They usually do not understand at first. But to stand by and passively allow them to continue on their path without attempting to correct is inexcusable.

Whether it's a coworker, an employee, a son or daughter, a sibling or a relative, you owe it to them and yourself to be respectfully straight. Since we are all terminal, it's the least we can do.

> *"How do you know what will happen even tomorrow? What, after all, is your life? It is like a puff of smoke visible for a little while and then dissolving into thin air"* (James 4:14–15, Phillips).

CAN'T WE ALL GET ALONG?

Season 8, Episode 3

SCENARIO

An enemy woman shows up at the 4077 to receive treatment. A South Korean Lieutenant named Park comes with his guards to question the woman and take her away as a prisoner. The doctors stall to prevent her from being released.

In the meantime, Major Winchester tries to distract the lieutenant in a game of chess while the other doctors plan her escape. She is caught and proceeds to spew her hatred of the American military. A dangerous confrontation erupts as the doctors try to resist the soldiers taking her away. At gunpoint, she is driven off to her fate.

OBSERVATION

Years ago, a man posed a legitimate question when he asked, "Can't we all get along?"

The answer is, "No, probably not." As individuals we might learn to respect each other and get along. However, when our core beliefs clash with the other person and what they represent, then it's best we go our separate ways.

Outside the help of a Higher Power, the chances for true reconciliation are slim and next to none.

So how do we proceed? Understand, disagreeing with someone does not have to make them our enemy. Unfortunately, it often does, since our objectives in life tend to be diametrically opposed. We keep it real when we support our cause the best we can without forcing others to change their beliefs.

> *"Do for others what you want them to do for you"*
> *(Matthew 7:12).*

CHANGE

Season 4, Episode 2

SCENARIO

Major Frank Burns is temporary commander of the 4077 after the death of Lt. Colonel Henry Blake. Frank takes the news of his replacement rather passively until alone with Margaret, then he goes into a full-rage tantrum.

The new C.O., Colonel Potter, is a career man who has had desk duty for the last two years. It is uncertain how he will do in O. R., but he passes the test.

Frank finally discovers that the new C.O. is quite tolerant of Klinger's cross dressing.

OBSERVATION

Many people are uncomfortable with change—some more than others. But change is inevitable, even in the workplace.

Getting used to a new voice or a different personality on the job is no small task. Just when we get comfortable with our boss, things change. The new person arrives, trying to prove himself while we try to figure out how to adjust to the incoming authority.

Some suggestions from a practitioner of change:

1. The sooner you realize the past is past the better you will be. A new way of doing things has arrived—get used to it.

2. You make the initiative to get to know the new boss—don't wait for them to adjust to you.

3. Decide to be loyal to your new supervisor. They will quickly respect your effort.

4. Avoid those who hold out on the new leader with their critical attitudes. It will not help their career.

5. Above all, do your job with as much enthusiasm as you can. It will improve your future and lift morale. You be the thermostat, not the thermometer.

"And whoever forces you to go one mile, go with him two" (Matthew 5:4, AMP).

CRISIS

Season 2, Episode 1

SCENARIO

Supply lines have been cut, causing the 4077 to be short of fuel, food, blankets, toilet paper, and no mail, to name a few. This hits the MASH unit quite hard as they already work under in a very spartan environment.

So the decision is made to go on Red Alert, which means rationing and conserving what supplies they have. Each officer is assigned an area to oversee. Officers and enlisted personnel double up on sleeping arrangements to stay warm, which causes additional problems.

OBSERVATION

While some people always seem to live from crisis to crisis, all of us have times when life gets out of hand. Income is reduced by loss of a job or physical illness. We cope and carry on the best we can, but reality sets in with too much month left after the bills.

What do we do when these times come? May I suggest we...

- Pull together with friends and family. Most of our acquaintances are willing and waiting to help, but we've got to let them know by swallowing our pride and communicating.

- Sometimes our lack allows our needs to be filled in other ways. Stay humble and open to creative provision.

- Times of difficulty afford us the opportunity to call upon a Higher Power. Whether you believe in God or not, this is an under-tapped resource that can curtail your crisis. It won't hurt to try it.

"And my God will liberally supply (fill until full) your every need according to His riches in glory in Christ Jesus" (Philippians 4:19, AMP).

DON'T BELIEVE EVERYTHING YOU READ

Season 10, Episode 13

SCENARIO

A famous war correspondent visits the 4077 with six pints of blood donated from people in the USA. A soldier arrives, having sustained injuries from wrecking his motorcycle. While BJ repairs the cycle, the writer calls in his overinflated story about the soldier who needed one of the pints of blood due to his heroic ride through enemy territory. Hawkeye is incensed with the untrue published article.

OBSERVATION

It has been said "don't mess up a good story with the facts." Embellishment tends to be part of the DNA of a good storyteller.

We live in a world of skewed, biased reporting. It is difficult, if not impossible, to get the straight scoop about the news, international relations and political issues. So, it is easy to rationalize what we share with others, be it written or verbal.

Truthfulness is a prerequisite for being believed. We may not be able to monitor others, but we can practice clarity of thought and veracity of delivery. Make the world a better place by staying believable.

> *"For we speak as messengers from God, trusted by him to tell the truth…" (1 Thessalonians 2:4).*

WHO GETS THE CREDIT?

Season 8, Episode 14

SCENARIO

Colonel Potter shares the good news that the editors of a medical publication in the States were impressed by the results of a delicate surgery performed by Charles and BJ. The two doctors are assigned to write a paper to be submitted. This is a great honor.

Now comes the problems—whose name shall be listed first? Who actually did the surgery itself and who only assisted?

After a lot of arguments, Colonel Potter steps in to remind everyone it was a team effort.

OBSERVATION:

Today, sports ads, especially on TV, tend to promote one player. It's as though a star player such as a quarterback single-handedly scores by themselves.

However, a quarterback is toast if not for a hardworking, talented offensive line who protects him from the other team. A pitcher is helpless without an effective catcher and a highly skilled infield and outfield who make him look good. A basketball player only scores with the team clearing the way.

It's like the story of the turtle on top of a fence post wondering how he got there. We know it was not by his own efforts.

It would benefit all of us to reflect regularly on where we are and the many unsung people who helped us achieve our goals.

All of us have supporters, both seen and unseen. We do more life together than we realize. We win more when we work and play together. Go Team!

> *"Humble yourselves before the Lord, and he will lift you up in honor" (James 4:10, NLT).*

TRADING PLACES

Season 10, Episode 10

SCENARIO

On Christmas Day British soldiers visit the 4077 and talk about their age-old tradition of having officers and enlisted personnel trade places on Boxing Day, the day after Christmas. So Colonel Potter allows his unit to try it out for themselves.

Early the next morning, all officers meet in the new temporary office of Colonel Klinger, who then assigns the staff their one-day jobs. Their perspectives change as they learn firsthand that the role of others is much harder than they anticipated. Enlisted staff also discover that the officers' lives are not as easy as they seem.

OBSERVATION

We look at others and think, "If I had their job, I could do it so much better." Truth is, we only see certain aspects of someone else's life, which tend to appear more glamorous than they are.
Equally faulty is to view certain jobs as too menial for us, not realizing that without the contribution of laborers, our role would be much harder and probably impossible to accomplish.

"Teamwork does help the dream work." The next time you are tempted to look down on or complain about your coworkers, don't.

> *"Just as there are many parts to our bodies, so it is with Christ's body. We are all parts of it, and it takes every one of us to make it complete, for we each have different work to do. So we belong to each other, and each needs all the others"*
> *(Romans 12:4–5).*

TIME TO CHOOSE

Season 10, Episode 17

SCENARIO

Hawkeye is called to an aid station on the front line to replace a surgeon temporarily. BJ returns to camp from some personal time away and immediately feels guilty since it was his turn, not Hawk's, to fill in at the very dangerous frontline clinic.

Upon Dr. Pierce's arrival at the dilapidated station, he finds only one doctor on duty, the other has been killed. Constant mortar shells drive Hawkeye under a table for safety. There he begins to write his will, seriously thinking about what he wants to leave with his dad and friends.

Meanwhile, life goes on at the 4077. BJ is worried sick that the dead surgeon might be Hawkeye. That worry is relieved when BJ discovers Hawk's stitching on a patient who came through the aid station.

OBSERVATION

Most of us have more possessions than we need. To plan and think about who we want to give them to seems morbid and unnecessary. "Yes, our time will come, but don't rush it."

So, what do you have that others would want or need? Things that mean so much to us might be useless to others. Clothes, pictures, even keepsakes may have no emotional appeal to anyone except us.

Our real wealth and value lie in our spirit and attitude. These are two priceless qualities unique to us which cannot be purchased. They are more "caught" than taught.

The most teaching any of us does is not in a classroom or formal setting, but just living life with our kids, family, neighbors and coworkers. This is why example is paramount. People primarily do what they see, not what they hear.

Our daily choices make a world of difference for us and for others.

> *"But if you refuse to serve the LORD, then choose today whom you will serve. Would you prefer the gods your ancestors served beyond the Euphrates? Or will it be the gods of the Amorites in whose land you now live? But as for me and my family, we will serve the LORD" (Joshua 24:15, NLT).*

FAREWELLS

Season 3, Episode 24

SCENARIO

Lt. Col. Henry Blake, first Commanding Officer of the 4077, gets word of his discharge while he is operating; he's going home. Everyone is thrilled for him as he says goodbye and prepares to leave. The chopper comes and the colonel is whisked away. A few hours later, Radar comes into the O.R. and announces that Blake's plane has been shot down with no survivors.

(Farewells of any kind are met with all kinds of emotions. The cast of *M.A.S.H* were not informed until just before filming that Col. Blake would die in a fiery plane crash. This made their acting all the more poignant.)

OBSERVATION

None of us know when we or someone we love will exit this world. Therefore, treating them with kindness and respect is so important, especially for those of us who continue to live on earth.

Don't delay your affirming words or helpful actions until the funeral. Give them now so others can receive them and be encouraged. This minor adjustment may help eliminate guilt and restore peace.

> *"So speak encouraging words to one another. Build up hope so you'll all be together in this, no one left out, no one left behind" (1 Thessalonians 5:11, MSG).*

FILLING BIG SHOES

Season 8, Episode 6

SCENARIO

Radar's uncle has passed away, which qualifies Radar as a hardship case—he goes home to help his mother run the farm in Iowa. This leaves the Company Clerk position open, which is a VERY important job in the operation of the MASH unit.

Klinger is chosen to replace Radar. However, the first few months are quite harrowing as everyone keeps comparing Klinger to Radar.

OBSERVATION

Even though Radar O'Reilly was of small stature, his responsibility was huge. Running the 4077's daily schedule, with all the unforeseen challenges, was daunting.

After many snafus and much criticism of the new man, it was decided that a period of adjustment was needed.

We live in a world conditioned to expect quick, if not immediate, results. It's easy to forget that it takes time to learn the ropes of anything, whether it be a beginning marriage, a different job or a new neighborhood.

In order to succeed, we need all the support and encouragement we can get. Likewise, the success of others can be greatly influenced by the consideration we give them. The Golden Rule of living never goes out of style.

"Don't pick on people, jump on their failures, criticize their faults unless, of course, you want the same treatment. That critical spirit has a way of boomeranging" (Matthew 7:1 MSG).

FUDGING THE NUMBERS

Season 9, Episode 16

SCENARIO

During a routine checkup, it is discovered that Col. Potter has high blood pressure. Having only a short time before retirement, the colonel tries to persuade Dr. Pierce to knock off a few numbers on the blood pressure test—no one will know. For once, Hawkeye is a stickler for regulations and refuses to fudge the numbers.

The colonel's medical condition is supposed to be kept a secret but ends up being circulated all over the camp. The very thing the colonel did not want happens as the staff goes overboard trying to improve the health of their leader by hiding the salt, monitoring the coffee, and sheltering the C.O. from stress. Their efforts fail.

OBSERVATION

Numbers do not lie. They can be misinterpreted and used by someone to promote an agenda, but they alone stand for objective truth.

There are times when we are tempted to alter the numbers or present them in a biased way. For example, we can set our bathroom scale a little lower to improve our day. We can blame our car's speedometer for allowing us to exceed the speed limit while radar says otherwise.

When it comes to our spiritual health, we do well to follow the Bible rather than our feelings or how well we compare with others. Our emotions constantly change and do not qualify by themselves to judge a situation. Coupling our feelings with objective truth (Bible) will help lead us to safety. Listening to God more than people always elevates spiritual health.

> *"And you will know the truth, and the truth will set you free" (John 8:32, NLT).*

TIERED MIRACLES

Season 11, Episode 2

SCENARIO

A patient refuses to eat, but Hawkeye finally gets him to talk. He had been in a foxhole with his buddies and fighting hard for many days. His C.O. arranged for a Thanksgiving dinner as a treat for his soldiers. This patient scarfed down his food and went back for seconds. When he returned, all his buddies were dead from artillery fire. He feels guilty, not deserving to live. Food makes him sick.

Another patient comes in with a toe tag indicating he is dead. The Father gives him last rites. While doing so, the chaplain notices a tear from the man's eye indicating he is still alive.

OBSERVATION

Most of us have an idea as to what counts as a real miracle. For sure, someone coming back alive after being pronounced dead qualifies because it cannot be humanly explained.

Others continue to breathe while experiencing the death of a relative or friend, the death of a relationship, or their joy has been killed by the prognosis of inoperable cancer.

Although we tend to rank miracles, when bad things happen to us we are not so discriminating. The willingness to go on after a life crisis with the help of a friend or professional is miraculous in itself. Do not underestimate divine providence intersecting your life.

> *"I know what I'm doing. I have it all planned out—*
> *plans to take care of you, not abandon you, plans to*
> *give you the future you hope for"*
> *(Jeremiah 29:11, MSG).*

THE SMELL OF MUSIC

Season 6, Episode 16

SCENARIO

After seventy-two hours in the operating room, the doctors are exhausted. Charles is playing his French horn to relax. His tentmates, Hawk and BJ, go on a shower strike to protest the major and his horn. The two unwashed docs go to breakfast and spread their stench all through the mess hall.

The standoff continues, forcing the stinky physicians to dine outdoors while Charles continues his serenading. Finally, the camp erupts and forcibly cleans Hawk and BJ with soap and a fire hose. Charles's horn is smashed by a well-placed jeep.

OBSERVATION

Where does our freedom end and the good of the whole begin? This is a matter that has perplexed humans since time began.

Operating in close quarters, whether it be in the home, factory, or office, compels us to give more than we take.

Question is, how do we do this? Seeing issues from someone else's viewpoint takes time and a change of heart. We were born with a selfish predisposition, which keeps us moving forward. However, how far do we go to get our way?

Experience teaches us that sometimes we need a third party to help us through sticky situations. Others can often see the issue better than we do. Our emotional investment clouds our perspective, so we tend to take a selfish route rather than the humble road. Although less traveled, the latter choice is the best one.

> *"Love from the center of who you are; don't fake it. Run for dear life from evil; hold on for dear life to good. Be good friends who love deeply; practice playing second fiddle"*
> *(Romans 12:9–10 MSG).*

I NEED YOUR HEP...

Season 10, Episode 6

SCENARIO

Col. Potter gets a notice reminding him of a speeding ticket he received while in town. So, he must attend remedial driving class as a penalty.

Even though tempted to "pencil whip" (to sign off but skip the class requirement), the Colonel goes ahead and takes the class. Led by Corporal Rizzo, a native of Louisiana, head of the motor- pool, who. as he would say, just wants to "hep" his commander.

The class is very elementary and boring so the Colonel sleeps through most of it. He is required to take a final exam and flunks.

A make-up test is allowed and to prepare for it, the Colonel requires Klinger to stay up all night helping him study. The Colonel passes, with help from the instructor, but, then there is the driving test. Klinger is half asleep as he walks back to the office and almost gets run over by the Colonel out on his road test.

OBSERVATION

All of us need help from time to time to navigate through difficult situations. Yet, we often just plow through thinking we can handle it ourselves. Truth is, we cannot get past life's curves without someone's assistance.

So, why do we keep trying to go it alone? We tend to see it as our responsibility even if we blame others. We know if we're to move on it's basically up to us.

Recognizing our need for help is the prerequisite for getting help. It's humbling to admit we cannot always accomplish everything on our own. Sooner or later an obstacle gets in our way which we cannot remove.

Receiving help brings closure and hope for the future. Getting back on track is usually a cooperative experience, not a solo event.

> *"If one person falls, the other can reach out and help. But someone who falls alone is in real trouble" (Ecclesiastes 4:10, NLT).*

IT WILL ALL WORK OUT

Season 10, Episode 22

SCENARIO

Hawkeye is charged with the monthly payroll distribution. However, he is interrupted by new casualties and has Klinger stow the unclaimed cash in a safe place. Unfortunately, Klinger's goat finds the money and eats it.

An army investigator comes to find out about the missing money. He does not buy the goat story and proceeds to write a report to his commander stating that Captain Pierce is responsible for the missing $23,000 ($256,000 today) and will have to repay it.

To prove the goat ate the money, a scheme is planned by Hawkeye and Col. Potter to pull the investigator away from his report with a fake phone call. Meanwhile, the goat is deliberately placed near the investigator's report, which now has molasses spread on it. Hawkeye and his accuser have to call a truce and cover for each other.

OBSERVATION

There is hardly anything in life worse than knowing the truth but not being able to prove it. Face it, the old excuse, "my dog ate my homework" is sometimes true. Logic says that it is highly improbable, but we know it happened.

So, how do we respond when we are in a similar predicament?

1. Understand, we live in an unfair world which, at times, seems to work against us.

2. Acknowledge that you may need outside help, paid or voluntary, to view your situation more objectively.

3. Take extra precaution to avoid negative input from media, social platforms, and people who don't believe in you.

4. Go slowly in reacting. Remember the quarterback option play that allows the passer to hold on to the ball long enough while the defense changes. Rest assured, it will all work out. Time and truth are on your side—embrace them.

"Trust GOD from the bottom of your heart; don't try to figure out everything on your own. Listen for GOD's voice in everything you do, everywhere you go; he's the one who will keep you on track" (Proverbs 3:5–7, MSG).

THE SAME TEAM

Season 6, Episode 12

SCENARIO

A visiting colonel is analyzing and predicting casualties, which makes Hawkeye mad.

An argument between Hawkeye and the colonel continues escalating until Dr. Pierce shoves the visiting colonel in a bar. The colonel brings charges against the doctor and a court martial is scheduled.

The colonel leaves but soon returns after being shot along the road. He has a change of heart and drops charges after seeing Pierce, along with other doctors and nurses, work so hard to save lives. The colonel realizes they all are on the same team.

OBSERVATION

It takes little effort to blow things out of proportion, especially as we deal with colleagues. What might seem so important and right is often disproved later when new information comes to light.

Someone said, "If you and I agree on everything, then one of us is unnecessary." Differences of opinion are a part of life. Adversarial relationships are counterproductive. We do not all have to take the same position to play on the same team. Diversity helps us all.

"Make every effort to keep yourselves united in the Spirit, binding yourselves together with peace" (Ephesians 4:3, NLT).

JUMPING ON THE WAGON

Season 8, Episode 16

SCENARIO

While receiving their monthly bar tabs, the doctors are amazed at how much they have spent, especially Hawkeye. So, Pierce announces he is going on the wagon for a week to see how he does without drinking.

The captain immediately becomes a nuisance and a pain in the neck to others as he changes to an early riser, gloating over his choice to become a teetotaler. He becomes testy with everyone, even with those who daily clean the patients' beds.

A near-death experience in O. R. reminds him of how precious life is and that we are not meant to judge others.

OBSERVATION

It is quite natural and so easy to preach to others about changes we make to improve ourselves, thinking everyone else must do likewise. It might be weight loss or a change of habits or what to consume. While our motive may be as pure as snow, it usually comes across to others as meddling or judgmental.

So what do we do? Modelling is a far better teacher than lecturing. Remember, you did not change overnight and others will not either. Patience with ourselves always precedes tolerance with those in our sphere of influence.

> *"Now may the God who gives endurance and who supplies encouragement grant that you be of the same mind with one another according to Christ Jesus" (Romans 15:5, AMP).*

5 'O CLOCK CHARLIE

Season 2, Episode 2

SCENARIO

The 4077 is sustaining daily bombings from a maverick, near-sighted North Korean pilot, referred to as 5 O'Clock Charlie. He flies by in his defective plane and attempts to hand toss a small bomb towards an ammo dump behind the hospital.

To combat the boredom, the camp bets on how close Charlie gets each day to his target. Upon the general's visit, Charlie gets lucky and actually bombs a jeep. Gung-ho Major Burns is granted his request for an artillery gun. The raids continue until the new gun gets lucky and hits the target that has been clearly marked by the doctors. Charlie flies away thinking he is a hero pilot.

OBSERVATION

There is a fine balance between ignoring potential threats and allowing them to control us, clouding our judgment. True, we live in a dangerous world and always need to be alert to our surroundings. We can think, *it will never happen to me or to mine*, but in our world of cause and effect, bad things do happen.

So how do we handle it? 4077 personnel made a social event out of Charlie's daily visits. They knew danger was in the air but chose to not overreact.

The problem worsened when medical people tried to become an artillery unit without any real knowledge of combat.

We often make things worse when we try to fight or even cope with life's difficulties just by ourselves. Instead of asking for help from "experts" we think we can do it, which often compounds the situation.

This episode reminds us to stay alert, but don't miss the show.

> *"If you want to know what God wants you to do,*
> *ask him, and he will gladly tell you, for he is always*
> *ready to give a bountiful supply of wisdom to all*
> *who ask him; he will not resent it"*
> *(James 1:5).*

THE RUMOR MILL

Season 10, Episode 4

SCENARIO

A general sends his emissary, Major Burnham, to the 4077 to check it out. Doctors and nurses think he is there to break them up to form other MASH units.

They want none of that, so they put on a charade trying to portray Col. Potter as old and decrepit. Meanwhile, Winchester is led to believe the major is scouting for a personal doctor for the general, so he tries to get close to the visitor.

When a huge wave of wounded arrives, the major sees the true 4077 kick into action as they heroically function like a well-oiled machine. Finally, it is revealed the real purpose of the major's visit: not to break up the MASH, but to copy it.

OBSERVATION

Assuming things often gets us into more trouble than we care to admit. Perhaps it's self-preservation or pride; nevertheless, it usually happens when we have only partial facts so we make up the rest.

Our assumptions can really go far afield as we envision

worst- case scenarios. This then leads us to act out, often contrary to our own nature. We can easily become paranoid, imagining endings never intended.

Our misguided behavior can usually be corrected by going to the person in charge and making an inquiry. Better to know than to assume.

> *"Don't grumble about each other, brothers. Are you yourselves above criticism? For see! The great Judge iscoming. He is almost here. Let him do whatever criticizing must be done" (James 5:9).*

GET BACK TO WORK

Season 7, Episode 19

SCENARIO

A young teaching doctor, Captain Simmons, visits the 4077 to instruct in new medical procedures when treating the heart. The surgeons are quite resistant to the suggested changes delivered by the brash, inexperienced doctor and let their feelings be known.

Col. Potter's phlebitis acts up, and the other surgeons insist he have bed rest. So Dr. Simmons steps into the operating room and shows he is a very good physician.

Winchester, who cannot deal with a "new guy in camp" who is as smart as he, gets drunk and cannot perform surgery for a while.

Finally, Col. Potter and Maj. Winchester rejoin the medical team although under great pain and distress. They resume their routines with a lesson learned that no one is indispensable.

OBSERVATION

Sooner or later, someone comes along who is as smart and efficient as we are and who will usually work for less pay. What do we do when something like this happens?

Oh, we may keep our job even though technology seems to be taking over. The question is: how do we endear ourselves to our employer?

Humans have attitude, but machines do not. Therefore, our consistent hard work ethic, along with a positive attitude, is very difficult to replace. Yes, we will be stretched and strongly tempted to walk away and never look back. But, longer-range thinking can help prevent that. The solution has and will
continue to be GET BACK TO WORK!

> *"Work hard and cheerfully at all you do, just as though you were working for the Lord and not merely for your masters" (Colossians 3:23).*

GROWING UP

Season 10, Episode 18

SCENARIO

In the chaos of promotion qualifications at the 4077, a new soldier comes in needing an operation. Col. Potter not only operates, but befriends the young man who is being bullied by two older guys. The young soldier never knew his real father.

To prove he is brave, the young recruit volunteers for EOD (Explosive Ordinance Disposal) training.

Col. Potter tries to dissuade the young man from pursuing EOD. Finally, Potter's advice is heeded and the soldier returns to his own unit.

OBSERVATION

Most of us probably would not want to relive our teenage years. Yes, we had fun times, but learning life's lessons can be costly. With the help of family and friends, most of us made it through the awkward years. But, with so many fractured families, not all kids survive, and are picked off by drugs and carelessness.

Positive role models are critical as we grow up. Making right decisions is more likely when we stick to our values, guided by the wholesome influence of others. Someone is observing what you do and how you do it. Being an example is par for the course.

We also grow up when we forget about ourselves and focus on others who are struggling. You can make a difference in someone's life right now.

> *"Overlook my youthful sins, O Lord! Look at me instead through eyes of mercy and forgiveness, through eyes of everlasting love and kindness" (Psalms 25:6–7).*

THE RIGHT TIME

Season 1, Episode 4

SCENARIO

Col. Blake appoints Capt. Pierce as chief surgeon of the 4077. Maj. Frank Burns is incensed and calls in Gen. Barker to observe the new chief surgeon. The Gen. arrives in the middle of the night, and the camp is definitely not ready for him.

Meanwhile, Hawkeye is involved in a poker game. While waiting for a patient to be ready for surgery, the general continually disrupts the card game, wanting a thorough explanation as to why the delay. The general finally joins the surgery team and gratefully learns some new techniques from Dr. Pierce.

OBSERVATION

Titles can really mess us up. When someone advances and we don't, even if they are far away and not in our sphere of influence, we can find ourselves wishing it was us and not them.

It's true, favoritism sometimes supersedes competence. The person making the decision for advancement knows or trusts someone else more than us. So, while they elevate, we remain where we are.

What do we do when this happens? Well, a person can leave and start over somewhere else, and that may be the right answer. On the other hand, if you choose to stay, your attitude and cooperative spirit will do more to change the mind of your boss than any kind of revenge you might plan. Getting along with others is a requisite for peace and stability. Don't destroy your future over current frustration. Time is the great equalizer.

> *"Quiet down before GOD, be prayerful before him. Don't bother with those who climb the ladder, who elbow their way to the top" Psalm 37:7, MSG).*

KEEP MOVING

Season 7, Episode 15

SCENARIO

Father Mulcahy is feeling down and discouraged, so he writes to his sister to explain his situation. He feels useless, even though he is attached to a hospital where soldiers are being helped every day. The doctors and nurses seem to make a difference by saving lives. However, the work of a chaplain is hard to measure and often feels meaningless.

The Father suggests to Radar to contact Winchester's mom to send him something for Christmas. She does so in the form of a red toboggan cap. This simple gift lifts the major's spirit and causes him to tell the Father how it saved him. The show finishes with the cease-fire being broken, bringing an end to the Christmas party in order to tend to the wounded. The Father comes to realize success is simply to keep moving.

OBSERVATION

Life is full of challenges, whether you work with people or machines. At the end of the day, you can usually see the results if you work in construction, on an assembly line, or in the arts. But working with people, while rewarding, is much harder to calibrate whether you are you making any progress or not.

Just like in steering a boat, forward movement is necessary if we are to move ahead toward our goals. Sitting still in the water may be serene and scenic, but it won't get you anywhere. Forward movement allows our sense of purpose to rejuvenate.

> *"I'm not saying that I have this all together, that I have it made. But I am well on my way, reaching out for Christ, who has so wondrously reached out for me. Friends, don't get me wrong: By no means do I count myself an expert in all of this, but I've got my eye on the goal, where God is beckoning us onward—to Jesus. I'm off and running, and I'm not turning back" (Philippians 3:12–14, MSG).*

THE LAW OF THE HARVEST

Season 7, Episode 6

SCENARIO

A medic named Jerry shows up at MASH 4077, not knowing where or who he is. Dr. Sydney Freeman is called in to help. Under hypnosis, the medic is subjected to a made-up battlefield scene. Jerry is trying to find his younger brother, but finally realizes his brother has been killed.

OBSERVATION

Dr. Freeman tells Jerry, "We're going to help you and you're going to help yourself."

We live in a world of needy people. It is also true that many of us like to help others, even though we often feel inadequate. The advice we offer is only as effective as the recipient's willingness to cooperate and change.

The Law of the Harvest says that what we sow in others will come back to us. Digging deeper, you will find that this law implies that if the one we are trying to help refuses to help themselves, then we move on to others who are ready to do their part to recover.

Do not feel guilty because you were not able to help someone. Be on the lookout for those who are committed to assist in their own healing.

> *"A time to tear, and a time to sew;*
> *A time to keep silence, And a time to speak"*
>
> *(Ecclesiastes 3:7, NKJV).*

THE RACE OF LIFE

Season 11, Episode 9

SCENARIO

The Chaplain of the 4077, Father Mulcahy, handles his stress by running. Klinger, who is always looking to make money via gambling, shares that a champion runner from Ohio State University has been assigned to their unit, so he tries to set up a race between the new recruit and a noted runner from another MASH unit.

The new runner arrives, but turns out to be the dad, not the runner himself. By this time the contest is afoot with doctors donating a week's pay to help stake it. The good chaplain is persuaded to run, but only if the benefits go to the orphanage.

An agreement is reached and race day comes. Obviously, the Father is totally outclassed by his highly talented, younger opponent. However, along the twelve-mile race the chaplain has opportunity to tell his challenger about the kids and how much they need a new roof and food.

The race is thrown and the kids get the much-needed supplies plus all the winnings from the betters.

OBSERVATION

What motivates you to step out of your comfort zone to help a cause bigger than yourself?

The ethics of this story hits each of us in different ways. However, the idea of using our blessings to assist others, especially children, is undeniably worthy of our time and resources.

Partial help is okay but often does not solve the problem. Giving without expecting a return is authentic and deserves our serious attention.

At the graveside service of a very wealthy man, two of the townspeople were talking. One said, "How much did he leave?" The other replied, "He left it all."

> *On my grandmother's wall was a plaque that said, "Only one life, twill soon be past. Only what's done for Christ will last." And so it is…"*

LEFT BEHIND

Season 11, Episode 15

SCENARIO

The staff of the 4077 begin discussing the idea of a time capsule. Margaret pushes ahead solo since her ideas are so different than that of the male personnel. She wants military items like an Army Field Manual included. The doctors want things like a Zane Grey novel, a bottle of cognac and bunion pads.

On the day of planting the capsule, the doctors show up with their own footlocker filled with memorabilia they would like to see included. Things like a broken fan belt to remember the hero chopper pilot who saved a life by flying two hundred yards at a time. The Chaplain offered boxing gloves to be used in the future instead of going to war. Even Klinger's silky black dress from his cross-dressing days made the cut.

OBSERVATION

Truth is, all of us will one day leave everything behind. The question is, Things that are important to you may not even register with someone else, including family. Opinions and preferences differ according to our personality and experience.

We are better off leaving some things behind. Things like bad memories, hurtful relationships and critical conversations contribute nothing to the people left behind. They are to be buried, but not in a place of remembrance.

The most important legacy we can leave is a clear picture of where we're going. The peace and comfort we want for our family and friends can be assured if they know we went straight to heaven.

THAT'S THE PROBLEM, WE DON'T KNOW

Season 11, Episode 5

SCENARIO

Captain Pierce dates a new nurse (Millie) and has a wonderful evening with her. The next morning at breakfast, Colonel Potter announces that Millie had been killed while accidentally stepping on a land mine.

Hawkeye volunteers to do the eulogy at her service. He inquires around to see if anyone really knew her. Apparently, she kept mostly to herself and did not interact much with the staff. She even was stingy with fudge she received from home, causing resentment from other nurses. We find out she was sharing it with the patients late at night.

Hawkeye reads her diary to discover Millie could not sleep after her date with him and had gone for a walk. She was an exceptional nurse even though shy.

OBSERVATION

There are people all around us who seem to live in the shadows. We see and hear them, but they are hard to know. They are often quiet by temperament, preferring to work alone. Competent, considerate, and calm seem to be their trademarks.

It is easy to misjudge someone when we don't know them and therein lies the problem. Waiting for someone to initiate and cultivate a friendship with us can be a long wait. It is incumbent on us to push back the unknowns and befriend folks who may be different from us. There's an old adage that says "if you want friends you gotta be friendly."

> *"A man that hath friends must show himself friendly, and there is a friend that sticketh closer than a brother" (Proverbs 18:24, KJ21).*

THE KIDS

Season 4, Episode 9

SCENARIO

The medical staff of the 4077 are coming off an extended session in the operating room when they hear that an orphanage has been bombed, forcing the kids to seek shelter, along with a very pregnant mother.

These precious, scared children arrive along with their caregiver, Nurse Cratty. Each of the staff is assigned a child or two to watch over while they are in camp. They are bathed, fed, and given medical attention. Bedtime stories are told as the kids fall asleep.

Selfish and insecure, Major Burns is only concerned for himself and his purple heart, which he received by embellishing a report. Meanwhile, the pregnant lady gives birth by C-section, but the baby has a nick it his butt from a gunshot. Frank's ill-gotten medal is awarded to the baby.

OBSERVATION

Most of us have never experienced the misfortunes of war. We see others suffer but feel powerless to change anything.

However, when it comes to children needlessly suffering, the unfairness of it all moves us and makes us want to jump in and help. We cannot sit idly by while innocent people are hurt in any way. Fortunately, there are many organizations already set up to assist people in need. They deserve and need our support.

The old adage "hear no evil, see no evil and speak no evil" has its merit, but sometimes we must speak up against those who abuse and take advantage of the system. In other words, wrong is wrong, and our silence can allow evil practices of others to continue causing more collateral damage to the most vulnerable in our world.

Karen Carpenter sang, "Bless the Beasts and the Children." The answer to this prayer usually involves humans. May we do all we can to be a part of that blessing.

> *"But Jesus said, Let the little children come to me, and don't prevent them. For of such is the Kingdom of Heaven" (Matthew 19:14).*

MOVING OUT OF OUR COMFORT ZONE

Season 3, Episode 19

SCENARIO

An aid station, situated on the front lines of the military conflict, requested a doctor, a nurse, and a corpsman to assist them until a new doctor could be assigned. Major Houlihan volunteers, and by a drawing, Hawkeye and Klinger are chosen. They go to the aid station and find the conditions to be very rough and unsafe due to constant shelling. The ram shackled building they work in has no roof and sanitary conditions are almost nonexistent. Trying to establish a safe, free of debris environment to work on each patient is impossible.

OBSERVATION

It's easy to be so absorbed in our current situation that we tend to complain about how rough we have it, that no one appreciates our level of sacrifice.

Much of the world would trade places with us in a heartbeat. Our minor inconveniences pale in comparison to the real-life suffering of millions of human beings.

What we take for granted would be luxuries for many people. Our working conditions, with all the built-in safety assurances are, for most people, totally unknown.

It would do us a world of good to move out of our comfort zone for a short while to personally see how others live and work. At the very least, it would reduce our complaining.

> *"No matter what happens, always be thankful, for this is God's will for you who belong to Christ Jesus" (1 Thessalonians 5:18).*

NEW WAYS OF SEEING

Season 5, Episode 3

SCENARIO

Hawkeye is asked to light a troublesome stove in the nurses' tent. It explodes in his face, so an ophthalmologist is brought in to treat the doctor's condition. A head wrap covering the eyes is applied and so he waits a few days to see if sight can be restored.

Meanwhile, Dr. Pierce has a whole new world open up as his other senses become more active. He hears a rainstorm and smells things, which helps him relate to others in a new way.

Finally, the bandage comes off and he can see again. As he views through a window to the outside, the 4077 has never looked so good.

OBSERVATION

Unplanned events like accidents, crime, weather, and illness impact all of us. While others care and try to help, there is only so much they can do, for their lives also face challenges.

So what do we do when part of our life closes down? As

humans we are not one dimensional, but have multiple assets at our disposal if we are open to them.

For example, I have been a speaker most of my life. When that avenue was reduced by retirement, I allowed writing to take center stage to continue forward movement. Reduction in one area can lead to expansion of another. Open your eyes and refuse to be blinded by the setbacks you experience. Insight comes after a decision is made.

> *"My brothers, I do not consider myself to have fully grasped it even now. But I do concentrate on this: I leave the past behind and with hands outstretched to whatever lies ahead I go straight for the goal—my reward the honor of being called by God in Christ" (Philippians 3:13–14, Phillips).*

OBLIGATIONS

Season 9, Episode 10

SCENARIO

Klinger leaves the clothes hamper out, blocking the aisle in the operating room, causing Major Winchester to trip over it.

As they clean up the area, the generator malfunctions, resulting in the autoclave (used to sterilize instruments) to build up pressure and explode.

Klinger sees the gauge rising and pushes Winchester out of the way, saving the major, but sustaining a broken nose from the blast.

Winchester, overcome with guilt, promises Klinger "round the clock" care for saving his life.

Klinger takes advantage of the situation. Winchester assumes Klinger's duties as Company Clerk. The major waits on Klinger hand and foot until he has had enough.

OBSERVATION

Some people live their entire lives under the operating principle "you owe me or I owe you." Sooner or later, we all find ourselves indebted to someone else we never can totally repay, but, we keep trying.

On the other hand, it is easy to milk the situation when someone owes us a favor, feeling obligated to us for our help, kindness, or financial assistance. We are tempted to take advantage of our debtor to get what is coming to us.

Getting even or ahead in this way is, at best, short-lived. Our initial help is nullified if we neglect to release them tangibly from their obligation to us. This simple act can free us from crippling emotions and restore wholesome relationships. Time to forgive and forget.

> *"Your heavenly Father will forgive you if you forgive those who sin against you" (Matthew 6:14).*

OWNERSHIP

Season 1, Episode 19

SCENARIO

It's the dead of winter in Korea and Hawkeye's father sends him a pair of long johns. Captain John McIntyre (Trapper), Hawkeye's best friend, feigns sickness, so Hawkeye loans him the johns. Trapper loses them in a poker game to Radar.

The johns continue to circulate throughout the camp, from the cook to Major Burns to Margaret, then Klinger to the chaplain, and then to Colonel Blake. Finally, Hawkeye gets them back.

OBSERVATION

The value of something increases when there is only one and we really want it. However, we tend to trade it for something we want more in the moment. In other words, our need for immediate gratification is short-lived as we move on to a new acquisition or adventure.

Coveting is as old as the Ten Commandments, where we're told not to do it. So how do we avoid wanting stuff others have?

    1. It's okay to admire and like the property of

others. It becomes a problem when we begin scheming to actually acquire someone else's possession.

2. Practice the art of being grateful for the good stuff that you have. Remember, most of the world would give anything just to live a day in your shoes.

3. Possessions are fleeting. They can all be gone in a heartbeat. It's all right to own things, just don't let them own you.

"You must not be envious of your neighbor's house, or want to sleep with his wife, or want to own his slaves, oxen, donkeys, or anything else he has" (Exodus 29:17).

PASSING THE BUCK

Season 11, Episode 14

SCENARIO

Colonel Potter returns to camp and questions Major Winchester about his assignment as Charity Collections Officer. Of course, the major forgot to get donations from all on payday, so now it becomes harder to get any help, even for a good cause.

Winchester bribes Margaret to take over his duties in exchange for a book in his possession. Margaret promises BJ to darn all his socks if he will assume collection duty. BJ threatens to reveal personal secrets on Hawkeye unless he becomes the official collector.

The job nobody wants finally comes to Father Mulcahy, who considers himself well suited for the job due to his years of raising weekly offerings.

OBSERVATION

In an ideal world every job would be filled with just the right person. Of course, we do not live on a perfect planet and often have to fill in and do tasks we are unsuited for since no one else will.

When you are called upon to do something or lead a

project for which you do not feel qualified to do, consider the following guidelines:

1. Your situation does not surprise God. He is prepared to help you not just to squeak by, but to do an excellent job.

2. Within you are untapped skills and talents that will be revealed as you move forward.

3. Allow the things you do well to propel you. For example, if you are a people person, then go all out to bring others in to help you. If you excel in numbers and detail, enhance these skills and get others to handle areas where you feel weak.

Through all of this it's quite possible you will discover gifts you did not think you had which can open up a whole new world for you. Give it a try. It's a win-win.

> *"It is God himself who has made us what we are and given us new lives from Christ Jesus; and long ages ago he planned that we should spend these lives in helping others" (Ephesians 2:10).*

TAKING ADVANTAGE

Season 6, Episode 9

SCENARIO

It was change day at the 4077, a day when old money or military script (currency used by military in Korea to pay soldiers and civilian personnel to keep US currency from inflating local economies of occupied areas) was exchanged for new bills.

Major Winchester, a wealthy surgeon from Boston, sees an opportunity to make a profit by buying up old script from neighboring merchants for ten cents on the dollar. This alienates the local people and blows up for the major as his scheme is discovered and stopped.

OBSERVATION

We do, in fact, live in an unjust world. Some people seem to "get all the breaks" or to "beat the system." This causes great resentment on the part of those who feel like they are being cheated.

Now, you may say, "I understand that this stuff goes on, but it does not impact me. I try to treat others fairly and mind my own business. That's good, isn't it?"

Consider, for a moment, how we treat those who serve

us in restaurants or anyone behind a counter. It is easy to take advantage of their situation, to be bossy and surly with anyone who fails to meet our expectations.

All of us can make a difference if we choose. While we cannot erase the rude behavior of others, we can balance the scales a little by tipping generously and being considerate with people who are just trying to help us. This goes a long way in this world and the next.

> *"So, chosen by God for this new life of love, dress in the wardrobe God picked out for you: compassion, kindness, humility, quiet strength, discipline. Be even-tempered, content with second place, quick to forgive an offense. Forgive as quickly and completely as the Master forgave you"* (Colossians 3:12–13, MSG).

THE BLAME GAME

Season 2, Episode 4

SCENARIO

Hawkeye and Trapper discover that shrapnel found in a Korean patient is from a USA bombing of a village named Taidung (Tie-dung). The doctors file a report to headquarters and a Major Stoner is sent to further inquire about the incident.

The major takes the shrapnel fragments with him, but nothing happens. A military newspaper, *Stars and Stripes*, reports the village was bombed by enemy fire.

The Army promises to rebuild the village, but the doctors also want the truth to be exposed. So the general makes a visit to the 4077 to urge the medical staff to just play ball, to stop making an issue about who did it.

OBSERVATION

The blame game is as old as Adam and Eve. For some it is a way of life. Just think how much better countries could run if we stopped blaming each other and own up to our own shortcomings.

The general wanted the doctors to do what would be good for the outfit, to take one for the team. However, cover up and diversion are never long-term solutions. Taking responsibility is the only way to right the ship.

So how do we decide the right thing to do in our lives? This is not easy, but sometimes we have to go along to get along. Standing on our own may feel righteous for the moment, but reality says we have to work with "the team," to get along with our family.

On the other hand, striking the right balance means truth cannot be sacrificed for the sake of expediency. Truth is, we need divine help to know when to hold and when to fold.

> *"If you want to know what God wants you to do, ask him, and he will gladly tell you, for he is always ready to give a bountiful supply of wisdom to all who ask him; he will not resent it" (James 1:5).*

THE CHALLENGE OF COMMAND

Season 7, Episode 1

SCENARIO

Colonel Potter is called to headquarters, so Captain Pierce is designated as temporary company commander.

In addition to his regular duties as Chief Surgeon, Hawkeye is immediately hit with problems of command, like filling out daily reports, ordering supplies and supervising his staff.

Hawkeye, who is always joking, is now loaded down with heavy responsibility, which he takes seriously. When BJ goes off to bring in a wounded soldier without asking permission, Hawkeye becomes furious, as he has been left short-handed with an influx of wounded. The colonel returns and orders Hawk and BJ to make up.

OBSERVATION

Being in charge sounds glamorous, but usually is not. Enforcing rules and managing people is seldom fun. People like to daydream about how much better it would be if they were running the show.

Leading any kind of organization, big or small, is

challenging. We won't really understand until we've experienced it. We are often too quick to criticize others who are in charge without knowing all the facts.

Passivity is not the answer. However, having empathy and understanding for leaders at work, in government, and even at home, is far more challenging than we can imagine. Time to lighten up!

> *"Here are my directions: Pray much for others; plead for God's mercy upon them; give thanks for all he is going to do for them. Pray in this way for kings and all others who are in authority over us, or are in places of high responsibility, so that we can live in peace and quietness, spending our time in godly living and thinking much about the Lord"*
> *(1 Timothy 2:1–2).*

HIDDEN HEROES

Season 10, Episode 19

SCENARIO

A famous middle-weight boxing champion visits the 4077 to build up morale. The camp goes all out to welcome the visitor, who then suffers a severe stroke while addressing the troops at a steak banquet.

Dr. Hawkeye Pierce handles the champ's case and shares the sad prognosis that the boxer is dying. Reporters swarm in and treat Hawkeye like a superhero as he monitors the irreversible situation of the champ. While Captain Pierce awkwardly handles the notoriety he receives from the media, Dr. BJ Hunnicut saves the life of another soldier in the operating room by using a crude prototype defibrillator on his heart—he literally brings the man back to life.

OBSERVATION

Fame and fortune tend to grab our attention, hindering us from seeing the bigger picture. We can get so enamored by celebrities and people of importance that we miss the everyday miracles that result from people doing their jobs.

Medicines that prolong and enhance our lives along with medical equipment are being invented and improved daily. Those who work behind the scenes, enduring frustration and approval delays are usually unsung, hidden heroes. They toil in anonymity.

Bottom line—they are heroes and so are those who assist them, families that sacrifice together time as their loved ones work overtime to complete a project (sometimes a miracle). We are blessed because of them.

> *"Don't just do the minimum that will get you by. Do your best. Work from the heart for your real Master, for God, confident that you'll get paid in full when you come into your inheritance. Keep in mind always that the ultimate Master you're serving is Christ" (Colossians 3:23–24, MSG).*

ONE STEP MORE

Season 8, Episode 1

SCENARIO

Clumsy Private Conway arrives at the 4077 needing medical help after falling into a foxhole.

Although a foot soldier, Conway likes to cook and makes Klinger a plate of Spam Parmesan. It is so good he begins to cook for the hospital rather than return to his unit on the front line.

Meanwhile, Colonel Potter is in a bad mood, having received a letter from his wife saying she misses him and is tired of living alone. Potter desperately wants to talk with her on the phone, but is unable to reach her. His frustration spews out on everyone else—he refuses to eat the new cuisine because he is worried about his marriage.

It is so obvious the foot soldier has been mis-assigned, but the Colonel misses it due to his own personal struggles.

OBSERVATION

Preoccupation with personal problems can cloud our ability to see clearly around us. Our behavior, while understandable, is often unjustified as we project on others our frustrations and unhappiness.

Our struggle usually impacts the workplace where we spend more than 33 percent of our day. Opportunities that would lift morale and improve conditions can be easily ignored when our focus is inward. We can alienate coworkers and impede progress by simply being self-absorbed.

Even with our current means of communication, we still struggle with understanding texts and email. We miss the tone of voice and can easily misinterpret the sender.

Face-to-face interaction is the best remedy to clear up issues. Second best is talking to the person on the phone to restore harmony and peace. So many problems can be solved by going one step more beyond our quick text or email.

> *"And if someone takes unfair advantage of you, use the occasion to practice the servant life. No more tit-for-tat stuff. Live generously"*
> *(Matthew 5:42, MSG).*

ENDNOTE

[1] Schuller, Robert H. 2005. Tough Times Never Last, but Tough People Do! Nashville: Thomas Nelson Publishers Nashville.

Printed in the USA
CPSIA information can be obtained
at www.ICGtesting.com
LVHW020713010224
770552LV00003B/13